PRIDE AND PERSISTENCE

STORIES OF QUEER ACTIVISM

PRIDE & PERSISTENCE
Stories of Queer Activism

MARY Fairhurst BREEN

DO YOU KNOW MY NAME?

Second Story Press

Library and Archives Canada Cataloguing in Publication

Title: Pride & persistence : stories of queer activism / Mary Fairhurst Breen.
Other titles: Pride and persistence
Names: Breen, Mary Fairhurst, 1963- author.
Description: Series statement: Do you know my name? ; 4 | Includes bibliographical references and index.
Identifiers: Canadiana (print) 20230198309 | Canadiana (ebook) 2023019835X | ISBN 9781772603491 (softcover) | ISBN 9781772603576 (EPUB)
Subjects: LCSH: Political activists—Biography—Juvenile literature. | LCSH: Gay activists—Biography—Juvenile literature. | LCSH: Lesbian activists—Biography—Juvenile literature. | LCSH: Gay rights—Juvenile literature. | LCSH: Sexual minorities—Civil rights—Juvenile literature. | LCSH: Social justice—Juvenile literature. | LCSH: Sexual minorities—Biography—Juvenile literature. | LCGFT: Biographies.
Classification: LCC HQ76.5 .B74 2023 | DDC j306.76/60922—dc23

Copyright © 2023 Mary Fairhurst Breen
Cover and illustrations © 2023 Katy Dockrill, i2iart.com
Edited by Brittany Chung Campbell

A version of the chapter "Post-Pandemic Pride: Natalie Moores" was published online by *Chatelaine* in 2022.

Printed and bound in Canada

Second Story Press gratefully acknowledges the support of the Ontario Arts Council and the Canada Council for the Arts for our publishing program. We acknowledge the financial support of the Government of Canada through the Canada Book Fund.

Published by
Second Story Press
20 Maud Street, Suite 401
Toronto, ON
M5V 2M5
www.secondstorypress.ca

In memory of Sophie Breen.

TABLE OF CONTENTS

PAGE 2   HISTORICAL TIMELINE: QUEER RIGHTS IN CANADA

PAGE 4   HISTORICAL TIMELINE: QUEER RIGHTS IN THE UNITED STATES

PAGE 7   PREFACE

PAGE 11   INTRODUCTION

PAGE 13   A GOOD ARGUMENT: SUSAN URSEL

PAGE 19   IT'S A BABY: ROGUE WITTERICK

PAGE 25   LAVENDER LIFE SKILLS: SPARKLE WILSON

PAGE 31   LOVE IS THE ANSWER: PATRICIA WILSON

PAGE 37   GOOD MEDICINE: ALI CHARLEBOIS

PAGE 41   A LOT OF THINGS AT THE SAME TIME: SUZE MORRISON

PAGE 47   TALENT AND NERVE: DEBBIE SHEPPARD-CHESTER

PAGE 53   ACTING OUT: JO VANNICOLA

PAGE 57   AN ALLY IN THE FIGHT AGAINST HIV/AIDS: DIDI CHARNEY

PAGE 63   DIGITAL DIVERSITY: RACHEL JEAN-PIERRE

PAGE 69   WE ALL NEED KINDNESS: FAITH NOLAN

PAGE 75   QUEER TANGO: ITZA GUTIÉRREZ ARILLO

PAGE 79   RUFFLING FEATHERS: TILLY KEEVEN-GLASCOCK

PAGE 85   POST-PANDEMIC PRIDE: NATALIE MOORES

PAGE 91 CONCLUSION

PAGE 93 GLOSSARY

PAGE 99 ACKNOWLEDGMENTS

PAGE 101 ABOUT THE AUTHOR

HISTORICAL TIMELINE

QUEER RIGHTS IN CANADA

1969

Homosexual acts are no longer a crime. Prime Minister Pierre Trudeau famously says, "There is no place for the state in the bedrooms of the nation."

1973

Pride Week is held in Vancouver, Montreal, Toronto, Ottawa, Saskatoon, and Winnipeg. This Canada-wide event for queer rights includes artistic events, dancing, picnics, and rallies for gay liberation.

1974

Adrienne Rosen, Pat Murphy, Sue Wells, and Lamar Van Dyke are arrested at a bar in Toronto for singing a song about being a lesbian. They become known as the "Brunswick Four" and their case echoes across Canada, raising awareness about homophobia and police brutality.

1977

Quebec becomes the first province in Canada to pass a queer civil rights law when it includes "sexual orientation" in its Human Rights Code.

1981

Two hundred police officers perform a coordinated series of raids on four bathhouses in Toronto called "Operation Soap" and arrest almost three hundred gay men. The Toronto Bathhouse Raids become a turning point for queer rights in Canada and spark protests for queer rights and against police brutality.

1981

The global AIDS (Acquired Immunodeficiency Syndrome) epidemic begins.

1988

Svend Robinson, a British Columbian Member of Parliament, comes out and becomes Canada's first openly gay MP.

1995

Sexual orientation is included in the Canadian Charter of Rights and Freedoms. This means discrimination against queer people is no longer legally allowed.

1995

Ontario is the first province to allow queer couples to adopt children, followed by Alberta, British Columbia, and Nova Scotia.

1999

The Supreme Court of Canada rules that a "spouse" can be a person of the same sex.

2002

The Ontario Superior Court of Justice rules that a boy—Marc Hall—has the right to bring his boyfriend to his (Catholic) high school prom.

2003

Ontario allows the first legal marriage between a same-sex couple.

2005

Canada passes the *Civil Marriage Act*, allowing all queer couples the right to marry. Canada is the fourth country in the world to do so.

2013

Kathleen Wynne is elected, becoming Canada's first openly LGBTQ premier.

2016

The Pride flag is raised on Parliament Hill in Ottawa for the first time.

2017

The *Canadian Human Rights Act* expands to protect people from discrimination based on their "gender identity" or "gender expression." This change is made to protect trans and nonbinary people.

2021

Yukon issues gender-affirming health-care policies, expanding medical coverage to a comprehensive list of procedures and surgeries covered by the government. It is the first of its kind in Canada.

HISTORICAL TIMELINE: CANADA

HISTORICAL TIMELINE

QUEER RIGHTS IN THE UNITED STATES

1962

Illinois becomes the first state to decriminalize private consensual sexual activity between two people of the same sex.

1969

Police carry out an unprovoked raid on a gay bar called the Stonewall Inn in New York City. Hundreds of queer people protest against this police brutality. This event becomes a turning point in the queer rights movement. Some of the leaders of the protest include Sylvia Rivera, Marsha P. Johnson, Dick Leitsch, and Craig Rodwell.

1970

On the anniversary of the Stonewall Uprising, the first Gay Pride marches are held in New York, Chicago, and Los Angeles.

1974

Elaine Noble is elected to the Massachusetts State House of Representatives, becoming the first openly queer person to be elected to a state legislature.

1978

The rainbow flag is flown during the Gay Freedom Parade in San Francisco and becomes a symbol of queer pride.

1979

Two men in California become the first same-sex couple to be allowed to adopt a child in the United States.

1981

The global AIDS (Acquired Immunodeficiency Syndrome) epidemic begins.

PRIDE AND PERSISTENCE

1985

The NAMES Project AIDS Memorial Quilt is conceived by San Francisco activist and author, Cleve Jones. It is composed of a patchwork of names of people who passed away from AIDS. Made of different materials, it weighs fifty-four tons, and it is the largest piece of community art in the world. Many people who died from AIDS did not receive proper funerals or burials, so the quilt is a way to remember and honor them and to fight against the stigma of this disease.

2015

In the case *Obergefell v. Hodges*, the United States Supreme Court rules that all states must allow same-sex couples to get married. The United States is the seventeenth country in the world to do so.

2003

The United States Supreme Court decriminalizes same-sex sexual conduct.

2004

Massachusetts becomes the first state to allow same-sex marriage.

2010

Don't Ask, Don't Tell is repealed, which means that queer people can serve in the United States military without having to hide their sexuality.

2016

The Federal District Court repeals Mississippi's ban on same-sex adoption, which makes it legal for queer couples to adopt children everywhere in the United States.

HISTORICAL TIMELINE: UNITED STATES

PREFACE

In 2021 and 2022, I interviewed a number of people whose lives intrigued or inspired me but who were, by many accounts, ordinary. From these interviews came the fourteen stories that make up this book. As they are all still alive, and range in age from their twenties to their seventies, I have only gone back in time as far as the early 1950s. Queer activism has brought major change since the middle of the last century, legally, politically, and socially (see Historical Timeline). Back then, it was illegal to be gay or lesbian in Canada and the US. You could even be fired from your job because you were queer—and many were. Each new decade has seen big differences in the daily lives of queer people in Canada and the United States, including the legalization of homosexuality in Canada in 1969, and in the US in 2003.

I have chosen to share the experiences of people who identify as women or nonbinary, and I'll explain why I use that language. Until recently, most people in North America understood there to be two genders: male and female. In fact, the idea of gender being separate from sex in mainstream consciousness is pretty new; we used to talk only about two sexes, based simply on a person's body. But, over time, people have questioned the idea that there are just two opposite genders. They have also challenged the idea that there are only two possibilities: straight or gay. So, when I talk about people who identify as women or nonbinary, I am including people who were born with female body parts and continue to identify as women, people who were born with male body parts and identify as women, and people who feel they have elements of both masculine and feminine.

What do we even mean by masculine and feminine, or male and female? Well, that's changing all the time too. In a way, we are going both forward and backward as some cultures have understood gender and sexuality more broadly long before now. For example, in many Indigenous cultures in North America, Two-Spirit people have existed for generations, long before the term was coined in 1990, and in fact long before colonization. Being Two-Spirit is not the same as being gay. It means being gifted with the embodiment of both sexes within one person. Those with this gift were traditionally considered balance keepers. What a beautiful way of putting it!

This book doesn't include the stories of people who identify as men. Why? Because historically there have been far more books, movies, songs, and artworks by or about men than anyone else, so you've got lots to choose from. I want to tell stories you haven't heard yet.

There are a lot of different words that have to do with gender and sexuality in this book. First, there is "queer," which is a fairly new umbrella term used to mean all the people who are part of the letters represented by the acronym LGBT (lesbian, gay, bisexual, transgender) and many more. LGBT became popular in the 1980s, when the words "gay" and "lesbian" weren't enough. More letters were added to include people who didn't neatly fit under L, G, B, or T. You will see "2S" for Two-Spirit, "Q" for questioning and queer, "I" for intersex, "A" for androgynous and asexual, and "P" for pansexual. In this book, you'll find different terms based on the storytellers' own words. You'll see both the word queer and different combinations of letters. It's worth noting that queer used to be an insult. You'll also read it in old books to mean simply "odd" or "weird." Sometimes it is powerful to take a word back and change its meaning from negative to positive. We're not done inventing and adapting language. That's the great thing about it—language is a living thing that can change alongside us.

In this book, you'll notice that I use the words gay or lesbian or other terms that may seem a little old-fashioned, but that's because the people I interviewed used these words when they told me their stories. These are their words, the ones they learned and became comfortable with during uncomfortable times in their own pasts. Again, the beauty of language is that we can choose how to use it as long as we do not disrespect others. At the beginning of each story, I note how people identify themselves. Some like to be called "she" and others like "they," which is either a plural or a gender-neutral pronoun. A lot of languages already have a gender-neutral pronoun. English doesn't, so "they" is a handy solution.

I have interviewed all kinds of really interesting people. Most are part of the queer community, and one is an ally. Some have done things specifically to improve the lives of queer people, while others are queer people who have done things to improve the lives of other communities or society as a whole. These stories show that everyone has the potential to make change in their own lives—and to make a difference in the lives of others.

—Mary Fairhurst Breen, 2023

INTRODUCTION

There have been queer activists throughout history. Many you may already know: Jackie Shane, Marsha P. Johnson, Edie Windsor, Sylvia Rivera, and Tegan and Sara. People who carved out paths where there were none, helping those who came after them. Individuals who challenged attitudes and stereotypes that did harm to members of the queer community.

So many queer people have had to live their lives in secret. Some still do. Others have been able to acknowledge and celebrate who they are and who they love. All the people you'll read about in this book have helped move us all toward greater acceptance, understanding, and joy.

Susan Ursel explains why she became a lawyer and how she uses the justice system to make change.

Rogue Witterick shares how they learned a different way of parenting from their own children.

Sparkle Wilson will inspire you with her enthusiasm for her work with queer youth in San Francisco.

Patricia Wilson tells the story of her transition from male to female back when almost nothing was understood about trans health.

Ali Charlebois talks about how much things have changed in the medical profession, and what still needs to happen.

Suze Morrison describes what it was like to walk into the Ontario Legislature at age thirty and try to be heard.

Debbie Sheppard-Chester's story takes us back to a time when queer people couldn't serve in the military, but she did it anyway.

Jo Vannicola is an actor and writer who shares their experience in the entertainment industry.

Didi Charney is an ally who did everything she could to support patients and educate the public at the beginning of the HIV/AIDS crisis in New York.

Rachel Jean-Pierre talks about why she switched from a career in social work to the growing field of digital marketing, and why diversity and inclusion matter in tech industries.

Faith Nolan recounts their life as a musician, using music to share messages of social justice.

Itza Gutiérrez Arillo describes the incredible feeling of queer tango, and how it helped them reconnect with their body.

Tilly Keeven-Glascock led a student protest that turned into a viral firestorm and shares what this taught her about activism.

Natalie Moores had a lot of time to reflect during the Covid pandemic and learned about her true self.

The activists in this book are no different from you. Many did not go looking to make waves, but their actions rippled out into the world. Small, everyday choices can be radical. You can start to change things just by making honest connections with yourself and others. Whoever you are, wherever you are, I hope the stories in this book make you think, "I could do that!"

A GOOD ARGUMENT

SUSAN URSEL

When I was growing up, the job options for women were secretaries, nurses, and teachers. I famously said to my mother when I was three, "I don't want to be a lazy mother when I grow up. I want to do something else." My mother thought that was hilarious, but it was mildly insulting, since she ran the household.

When she was a kid, Susan Ursel's teachers said she'd make a good lawyer. "I like to argue a lot. I come from a feisty bunch of people on both sides of my family. In high school, I used to debate other students into the ground." She started university planning to become a journalist, but it turns out her teachers were right. The courtroom is where she belongs.

Susan's mother had an entrepreneurial spirit. But, like many middle-class women of her era, she was stuck being a homemaker. After Susan and her siblings were grown, her mother started a floral business. She and her flowers blossomed. Susan witnessed the value of work, especially for women, and how happy it made her mom to work and earn for herself.

Susan was also aware, even as a teenager, that a lot of people had unfair or unsafe working conditions. She read about the mass boycott of California grapes and learned about union leader Cesar Chavez. The farm workers were striking for decent wages. Even though she was a kid and didn't have a job of her own, she wanted to do something.

> Every Saturday morning, I dutifully picketed the local Dominion store, much to my parents' embarrassment. I listened to what people were saying about [their] working experience and I saw my mom being excluded from the world of work. That's really what made me want to become a labor lawyer. I saw work as such a fundamental human right.

Over time, Susan also began to focus on LGBT rights. It's important to remember that until the tail end of the last century, no one really talked about queer people or the issues affecting them. Susan remembers,

> I tried to be a nice straight girl from the 'burbs. It was not very successful or convincing to anyone. As usual, everyone was way ahead of me. Eventually, I came out in my twenties, and immediately I understood the connection between my personal

life and my human rights. Being myself and fighting for our community were mixed up together for me.

Some Canadian laws had changed to give Susan better protection as an individual. She couldn't be fired just for being a lesbian, for example, but she still couldn't legally marry a woman. The law hadn't caught up to the way queer people were living their lives as couples and families. There were big problems about who was considered a legal spouse and legal parent. For example, if you were sick, your same-sex partner might not

Susan URSEL

- pronouns: **she/her**

- self-identification: **lesbian**

- works as a lawyer focusing on **labor** and **employment**

- won a **landmark victory** for queer education at the **Supreme Court of Canada**

have the right to visit you in the hospital or consult with your doctor. Only married spouses were each other's "next of kin." If you were a kid with two moms, the school might only recognize one as your parent. The other was treated like a nobody. She might not be allowed to pick you up from school or sign permission slips for you to go on class trips. Imagine being told, "That's not your real mom" or "That's not your real dad." Once again, Susan needed to do something about it.

Susan has been involved in a great many legal cases in support of same-sex marriage and equal rights for families. One of Susan's most interesting cases started with a kindergarten-Grade 1 teacher from Surrey, British Columbia in the 1990s. Mr. Chamberlain requested three picture books for his classroom library, each with same-sex couples. The school board refused to approve them on the grounds that parents might object and kids this young didn't need to know about nontraditional families. Mr. Chamberlain argued that he, like every other teacher, had kids in his class who had two moms or two dads, or a single queer parent. Others had a gay uncle, a lesbian cousin, a gender non-conforming neighbor, or maybe wondered if they were growing up to be queer themselves. There was no reason the families in the books they read shouldn't look like their own families. The same argument had been made in the 1950s and 1960s, when some people opposed books with non-white characters in schools. That seems ridiculous now, doesn't it? Well, books with only straight people posed a similar problem.

The Surrey school board wouldn't budge, but Mr. Chamberlain wasn't done fighting. Instead, he took the board to court for the right to have queer books in his class. The case went all the way to the Supreme Court of Canada, the highest level of court in the country, where Susan was one of the lawyers who presented her argument to the panel of judges. She stood up and said, "I'm here to speak for the children." The judges started to see the point: There were real children being affected by this rule in real classrooms. No one wanted to discriminate against kids or make school harder. No kid should feel left out. Susan's baby daughter was in the court that day with her other mom.

The judges agreed that the books kids read at school can and should include characters that reflect the people in their worlds. Chief Justice Beverley McLachlin dismissed the board's concerns that children would be confused or misled by classroom information about same-sex parents. She wrote: "Tolerance is always age-appropriate, children cannot learn unless they are exposed to views that differ from those they are taught at home." Susan notes with a smile that the books Surrey banned are celebrated as classics now.

Susan is honored as a trailblazer in the legal profession. She didn't think about whether she was blazing a trail while she was doing her work. It's only when you look back that you can see how today's laws were built on earlier changes to unjust ones. The things we take for granted—from our right to marry the person we love to the stories we find and share in our school libraries—took a lot of effort by a lot of determined people. Big shifts start with small steps that happen in families, classrooms, and neighborhoods. Anyone of any age can take those first small steps!

Susan says that when she's fighting a tough case, she often imagines her mother, grandmother, and earlier ancestors touching her shoulders, giving her encouragement. Susan is over sixty now and as excited as ever about her work. For her, being a lawyer means taking a bad situation and making something good come out of it.

IT'S A BABY

ROGUE WITTERICK

We're going to listen continuously to actually know who this person is.

"Boy or girl?" people ask when a baby is born. For a long time, nobody questioned this. It seemed like an important detail. In fact, it was very important, if you happened to be a British princess. Until 2011, only boys could be heir to the throne (unless the king had no sons, which is how Queen Elizabeth II got the gig). Princess or not, if you were born a girl in Canada before 1929, you were not technically a "person" under the law.

The definition of persons under the *Constitution Act* of 1867 was understood to mean "men." This definition was challenged in the Person's case when the Famous Five (activists Nellie McClung, Louise McKinney, Henrietta Muir Edwards, Emily Murphy, and Irene Parlby) successfully pushed back against the laws to allow women to be appointed to the Senate, one of the highest political roles in Canada. Senators approve laws and have a say in national issues. The Person's Case opened doors to politics and power over the next century. But change is slow. It took decades before women were able to open a bank account, get a credit card, or apply for a mortgage. Imagine if there were only women in your family. What would you do? Throughout history, the sex of a baby has determined a lot more than the color of their onesies. (And even today, if you want to buy a onesie, they come in drab neutrals for boys and pink for girls.)

These days, routine ultrasound pictures can show a baby's sex organs while it's still in the womb. Some parents want to know, others don't. And some parents throw what they call "gender reveal" parties. (This term is wrong, by the way. You can only ever know the sex of a baby at birth, not the gender. "Gender" is a twentieth-century word to describe how a person feels and wants to be understood. It refers to their identity, not just a reference to their body parts.) Rogue Witterick and their partner David went the opposite direction.

Rogue and David believe in democratic parenting. Rogue explains, "All of my living has been about how we can be in community and support each other in becoming our most authentic selves." As a parent, Rogue feels their job is to "facilitate becoming" for their children. Practically, it means giving their children a voice in all the decisions that affect them—what to wear, which toys to play with, where or whether to go to school, or what kinds of activities to do. Rogue spent many years working in child and youth advocacy and delivered training focused on respecting the dignity of children. At the time, they weren't a parent yet, and people would remark, "Well, it's easy for you to say all this, but parenting really puts your ethics and social justice work on the line. It brings it not just close to home, but into your home." When they had their first child, Jazz, they wanted to apply their knowledge about child development—"to walk the talk," as Rogue puts it.

Rogue WITTERICK

- pronouns: **they/them**
- self-identification: **queer** and **nonbinary**
- worked in **youth advocacy**
- based on their experiences with their first two children, **chose not to assign** their third child a **gender at birth**

Jazz had a very clear sense of who she was from the beginning. Rogue was in awe of this kid who could express what she wanted and needed better than Rogue had ever been able to do. She taught Rogue a lot. By the time Jazz was two, she was making choices about how she looked and behaved that were pushing against gender stereotypes. Her parents were committed to expanding notions of what boys and girls can be and do. But it hadn't occurred to them to call Jazz anything other than he/him at that point. Jazz's sibling Kio came along, and their parents continued to give them the freedom to express themselves any way they liked. They felt all kids could be many things: loud, shy, fast, imaginative, or stubborn. David and Rogue both identify as queer; they may look like a straight couple, but they don't feel they belong in that category. More importantly, they really don't like categories.

By the time baby Storm was due to arrive, it was clear Jazz was a trans kid. She was the age to start school, but decided she wasn't going anywhere she wouldn't be accepted as herself. The family opted for homeschooling. Jazz asked her parents, "Are you going to make the same mistake again?" Meaning, "Are you going to decide whether the baby is a boy or a girl right away? Or are you going to wait and see who the baby really is?" They chose not to reveal the sex assigned to Storm at birth. More than ten years ago, this was an unusual path to take, although other activists had begun paving the way. They knew it would be uncomfortable and challenging. They knew they would face questions both from strangers and from people they knew. But they were determined to break out of the boy/girl system.

Some friends and family were all in favor. Others were confused. They seemed unsure how to love a baby if they didn't know what it was. Rogue and their family explained over and over that it was a baby. A baby is a baby. Go ahead and love it all up! Make faces and play peek-a-boo and talk in funny voices. Why was it more complicated than that? It was never the plan to go public with their decision. But one day someone asked the inevitable question, "Boy or girl?" And David explained that they didn't know yet. It was strange enough that word spread, and before long, the *Toronto Star* came looking for a story.

The family decided to welcome the journalist, to explain their decision in the hope it would open people's minds. They thought a little article would appear in a back section of the newspaper, something a few people would read over their morning coffee. Perhaps some would even see the sense in this approach: let every person decide for themselves who they are. Instead, the story was a huge feature in the Saturday edition—the biggest day for newspapers all week. Rogue was out for a walk with Storm when they passed a newspaper box. Inside was a great big photo of the baby on the front page.

The response was immediate. The story was the most popular item the *Toronto Star* had ever published. The article itself was neither positive nor negative. But other media outlets picked it up, and soon the headline "Storm of Controversy" was all over the news. Rogue and their family were unprepared for the attention and criticism. Everyone seemed to have an opinion on their family, wherever the story traveled.

Some people reached out to offer their support and friendship. Others thought the family was just seeking the spotlight. Outrage was directed at Rogue. As Storm's mother, they were held responsible for this social "experiment." The same outrage was not directed at David, though there was some, as Storm's other parent. The criticism got so fierce that a group formed to lobby child services to take the children away from Rogue and David. Rogue was fired and had to take a different career path. People yelled at the family in public, and some days it became scary for them to venture outside. The family was urged to talk to the media to defend themselves, but they refused. Their priority was to protect their children, and they did not want to feed into the frenzy.

People kept talking and, over time, the tone changed. Attitudes shifted as gender nonconforming people felt freer to be open about who they were and how they felt. The queer community welcomed conversations about gender-open parenting. The focus shifted away from baby Storm to include the well-being of all kids who don't fit into traditional gender roles. Awareness of the needs of trans kids grew, especially as research drew attention to the risks they face from violence or self-harm. The more open and understanding we are as a society, the safer people feel to love themselves. Now, more young people are letting go of old categories to just be themselves. A baby is a baby, a kid is a kid, a person is a person. Public opinion is catching up with Rogue and their family.

POSTSCRIPT

In the years between 2011 and 2021, many more parents have embraced the idea of leaving gender up to their children. There is even a catchy name for these babies: "theybies." Organizations and online forums offer advice, support, and resources for parents of theybies.

Val Colden, a Canadian parent of a baby born in 2021, says, "I wanted to give Reese the freedom to figure out who they are without being put into a box based on their perceived gender. I don't think babies really develop gender until they are two or three years old, anyway." Val had a much smoother experience than Rogue. Her parents were a bit concerned but have embraced her decision. Val was pleased to see that when she filled out the form to name who gave birth to Reese, she had the choice of "mother," "father," or "parent." This shows an understanding that not only women get pregnant and give birth. Some jurisdictions have begun allowing people to choose "M" for male, "F" for female, or "X" for nonbinary on their birth certificates. Other pieces of identification, like driver's licenses and health cards, are getting rid of the M/F boxes altogether. What difference does gender make when you're asked to prove that you're old enough to drive or buy beer? Sometimes change is very slow, but for kids born in the past decade, it has moved pretty fast.

LAVENDER LIFE SKILLS

SPARKLE WILSON

I have always been someone who volunteers or signs up for a project or group that sounds interesting or that I think would be a fun new experience for me. As an adult, I'm very aware that this trait of mine has been a great asset to me. Without it, I would have missed out on so many connections and experiences that have led me to where I am today. I know I would not be the person I am without the many people who have invested in me as a person in the many programs and internships I have been in.

Sparkle Wilson was an adventurous kid, always up for new things. As soon as she was old enough, she liked the independence of earning her own money. When she was in high school in her hometown of San Francisco, she heard about a group called LYRIC (Lavender Youth Recreation and Information Centre). She agreed to go with a (closeted gay) friend to check it out. She was intrigued by one of their youth internships: a paid program called Summer in the City. It offered life skills, job training, and a window into queer history—topics usually left out of her school curriculum. She signed right up—and loved it. Sparkle returned to LYRIC in her later teens as an alumni youth educator. She led a group called Honey for Black and brown femme queer teenagers.

In San Francisco and other American cities, paid internships are popular and very competitive. They help youth gain skills and experience while making some money. In Canada, youth are more commonly urged to volunteer; in some provinces, a set number of volunteer hours is required to graduate from high school. Paid internships are rare, even among university students and graduates. Many argue that this unpaid work exploits young people. It widens the gap between those who can afford to volunteer, and those who have to take whatever jobs they can get to support themselves or pay for their education.

Sparkle called herself an "enthusiastic ally" to the queer community as a young teen. She now proudly identifies as a Black femme and happily lives under the big, inclusive tent that is queerness. She explains her evolution:

> When I went back to work at LYRIC, I would tell the youth that there isn't a need to figure things out right away, or that you may never need a "label." I realized I was telling them things I also needed to hear. I work with youth of all races and backgrounds, but I always form a special connection with my Black femme youth. They always tell me how much they treasure their relationship with me because I "get it." I say "femme"

because I also work with trans Black girls and I don't want to exclude them. I am aware that I am a cisgendered Black woman and have a little bit of privilege that comes with that compared to trans women.

After high school, Sparkle studied social work and psychology. She worked part-time with youth in the foster care system. Her job was to support youth who had just been removed from their families before being placed in a foster home. It was rewarding but draining. She was meeting these kids on one of the most difficult days of their lives. Sparkle wasn't really looking for a new job, but she noticed that LYRIC was expanding and hiring.

Sparkle WILSON

- pronouns: **she/her**

- self-identification: **queer Black femme**

- yes, **Sparkle** is her real name!

- works with **LGBTQQ+** and **ally youth** to build leadership and community

LYRIC began as a grassroots project in 1988. Its goal was to help LGBTQQ+ youth connect in a safe space, where they could be themselves and make friends. The organization grew, creating an education program on sexuality and gender. It kept growing to meet the needs of youth, eventually getting the funds to buy a big purple building in the Castro area of San Francisco—the most famous queer neighborhood in America. LYRIC is always evolving to add more programs to support queer youth and to provide education about LGBTQQ+ issues within schools and the broader community.

The internship program Sparkle attended has expanded. The Sequoia Leadership Institute (named after drag star Ms. Sequoia, who worked at LYRIC at one time) continues to offer paid scholarships for LGBTQQ+ youth and allies.

The LYRIC website explains its mandate: "Real work experience, community building and skills for life come together to support LGBTQQ+ and ally youth to step up as leaders and designers of lasting social change."

LYRIC also offers all kinds of groups to connect and support trans youth, youth involved in sex work, BIPOC youth, and more. It offers assistance with legal issues, housing, and health. It has become a place where queer youth can go to find help with whatever they need.

Two years after being hired by LYRIC as a youth advocate, Sparkle became the program manager of the Sequoia Leadership Institute. You can hear the excitement in her voice when she describes her work. And no wonder! Her program brings together so many great elements. Young people learn very practical "adulting" skills, like banking, budgeting, and time-management. They learn how to write cover letters and résumés, and handle job interviews. It's hard work, but it's all integrated into a group project the youth choose and plan themselves. It might be an art show, a community garden, a neighborhood walking tour, or a big dance party. Queer history and culture are celebrated in everything they do. They have fun, and they also tackle serious issues, including anti-Black racism and white supremacy. They learn to think critically, to question, to collaborate, and to advocate for themselves. Sparkle calls them her young "social justice warriors."

In summer 2021, a group of youth interns created an online resource called Dorothy's Dictionary, a name that comes from the old phrase "a friend of Dorothy," which means a queer person. They looked at historic firsts in queer history and at the evolution of language to describe gender and sexuality. They also wrote up a handy list of rebuttals to common misconceptions and questions, such as:

Why are there so many more gay people nowadays?
Gay people have always been here. We just don't have to hide anymore.

No one is born gay!
Sexuality is never a choice, nor is it a mental illness.

Why are y'all making up a million genders?
Gender is a social construct. If there was no society to tell us how to behave based on biological makeup, the concepts of "men" and "women" would be void. Nonbinary genders are not new and have existed for hundreds of years in many cultures.

Gay people have the same rights as everyone else.
Only twenty-nine countries worldwide allow same-sex marriage. Seventy-nine countries criminalize queerness. Queer youth are five times more likely to die by suicide than straight youth. In the US right now, states are putting forward bills to remove existing rights.

Letting kids transition is harmful.
This fearmongering is baseless. Doctors do not perform surgery on people under eighteen. Hormone blockers are reversible. The best thing parents can do is support their kids, use their preferred pronouns, and let them dress as they like.

LYRIC is always growing and changing. Right now, it is raising funds to expand its space. As well as running programs, Sparkle is heading up a Youth Leadership Council that will give youth a place on the organization's board of directors. This is an important step for any agency serving youth. If they don't have a seat at the table, they don't have a say in the decisions that affect them.

Because LYRIC's programs welcome queer youth *and allies*, the teens who attend don't have to be out. This strategy has made it easier for youth to participate. If they are under eighteen, they need their parents' permission, but Sparkle says families are generally happy to have their kids attend, even if they

LAVENDER LIFE SKILLS: SPARKLE WILSON

need a bit more time to warm to the idea that their kids might be queer. She is always glad to see lonely youth find their community and find their voice. Often the conversations are so lively, it's hard for her to get a word in to say it's time to wrap up and go home! When kids graduate from their internship, there are always lots of happy tears.

LOVE IS THE ANSWER

PATRICIA WILSON

*There's a good chance that if I hadn't transitioned, I would have died.
I had to transition in order to carry on.*

Patricia Wilson has been called the "guardian angel" of Buddies in Bad Times Theatre. Buddies is the world's oldest queer theater with its own venue, founded in Toronto in 1979. For decades, Patricia supported and mentored young queer adults from behind the bar in the room known as Tallulah's Cabaret. There is a stereotype that people like to tell bartenders all their troubles, and Patricia has always been an active and willing listener. She's always dressed in badass black rocker clothes, yet she calls most everyone "honey." The Toronto queer community knows her from Buddies, from her music or writing, or from her daily social media posts. CBC Arts called her "an iconic Facebook writer" for her online words of wisdom and kindness.

Patricia was born with male sex organs and went to an all-boys school in Windsor, Ontario. She had a happy childhood full of friends and activities she enjoyed. By high school, though, she felt different from other kids. She says, "I was looking for a crowd to be part of, and it happened to be the drug crowd. It was a party of misfits."

In the late 1960s, the hippie movement was sweeping across North America. Hippies opposed war and violence. They wanted freedom from the strict social rules of the 1950s, when men were supposed to make money and women were supposed to raise children. They saw nothing wrong with sex before marriage and believed that some drugs could help people relax and think more clearly. During this time, illegal drug use became much more common among teens and young adults. It's important to note that most of the drugs available at that time were far less toxic and dangerous than illegal drugs today. The risks then and now are vastly different.

Patricia quit school in Grade 10. From that moment on, she worked in construction. She presented herself as a male but knew that's not who she was. This was forty years ago. Patricia didn't have the language to describe what she felt. The word "transgender" didn't even exist until 1965. Many people were not used to the idea that sex and gender were two different things. Patricia couldn't see any path forward. She says, "You didn't talk about it to anybody. It just wasn't done."

By her twenties, Patricia knew she couldn't keep living as a man. She had to make the leap. She got up the courage to talk to her doctor, who sent her to the Clarke Institute in Toronto (now part of the Centre for Addiction and Mental Health or CAMH). She had three days of psychological testing, staying in a hotel by herself, telling no one. Patricia knew she would face rejection from family members and sadly, she was right. Her mother didn't accept her until she was older. Her sister talked her mother into changing her outlook. Fortunately, Patricia says, "As we get older, our mind changes. We're always growing."

Patricia WILSON

- pronouns: **she/her**
- self-identification: **trans woman**
- **musician** and **poet**
- **mentors** and **helps** queer young adults

The Clarke Institute has been criticized by the trans community for its past approach to gender identity. It earned the nickname "Jurassic Clarke" for its treatment of trans patients and for other controversial research claims it made during the 1960s and 1970s. At the time, transgender people were very poorly understood. Medical books would have described Patricia as having a "psychosexual disorder." Patricia recalls that the doctors there certainly did not encourage transitioning from male to female, but she convinced them it was necessary. She managed to prove to them that she could not have a healthy life as a male but would be a contributing member of society as a woman.

She fought for and received the medical care she needed. She had to travel to the United States for surgery, but the cost was covered by the Government of Ontario. At the time, it was called a "sex change operation." Now it is called "gender-affirming surgery." Some trans people choose top surgery only (adding

LOVE IS THE ANSWER: PATRICIA WILSON **33**

or removing breasts), some choose bottom surgery (changing genital organs), and some choose neither. These surgeries are personal choices to help people feel more comfortable in their bodies.

Once Patricia decided to transition, she took a huge risk.

> I was a welder in a factory. I left on Friday as a male and came back on Monday as a female. I had told my boss I was going to do this, but my co-workers had no information and no concept of what was going on. We all had a meeting about it. I was treated terribly, of course. I knew if I survived that, I could survive anything.

When the harassment became too much, Patricia quit, took some time off, and then made a career change. She became an arts administrator and helped save the beautiful old Capitol Theatre from demolition in Windsor. She hoped she would be given the job of running the theater, but she was turned down. Windsor was not a queer-friendly town. As far as she knew, Patricia was the only trans person there. People were mostly confused by her, if they noticed her at all. Patricia got a job as a lighting designer at that same theater and met a singer named Hélène. They have been a couple for thirty years.

Together, they moved to Toronto. Patricia was offered a job at Buddies in Bad Times Theatre as a publicist. By this time, she had attended university as a mature student, majoring in literature and philosophy. She had heard about Buddies; a theater artist she met in Windsor told her it would be the perfect place for her. She had seen one of Buddies' wild floats at the Pride Toronto parade. It looked like a band of rowdy pirates, and she thought, "That's the ship I want to be on!" When Buddies moved into a new, bigger building with a cabaret space and bar, Patricia became its bartender, a job she held until the age of sixty-seven.

Things are obviously different for trans people today than they were for Patricia. But she cautions that transitioning does not mean things will instantly get better. She states frankly, "It is the hardest thing in the world." It is still true that people who don't easily "pass" as the gender they identify with have a hard time. And the problems they had before transitioning—especially alcohol or drug dependence—are likely to worsen. She advises young people to take care of their emotional health every step of the way and find support where they can. "I make sure they understand that for everything that makes them feel different from everyone else, there are more things that are the same."

As an adult, Patricia has returned to the music she loved as a kid. She's the guitarist in a rock band and performs as a studio musician. Patricia has also published some of her writing, both poetry and personal essays. As she ages, she is very clear about her priorities. Her home life is number one. She cherishes her relationship with her partner and nurtures it. Patricia ends her popular Facebook posts with the words she lives by: "Enjoy the moment and be kind when you can."

GOOD MEDICINE

ALI CHARLEBOIS

Often LGBTQ folks have negative experiences in health-care settings and feel they have to hide elements of themselves. One of the joys of my work is being able to provide a safe space where people know that I understand a bit more about their lives, and that I won't make silly assumptions about who they are, who they love, and what they do.

Ali Charlebois studied psychology in university thinking it would be her career path. But she realized there was a problem with the way mental health care is provided in Canada. Psychotherapy, also called "talk therapy," usually costs money. Ali didn't want to help only those who could afford to pay, so she applied to medical school to become a psychiatrist. Then her interest shifted to family medicine. She remembers, "I had a formative experience when both of my parents had cancer. I learned what a positive impact a good family doctor can have. And in family medicine, you can still do a lot of mental health work."

It's not easy to find a family doctor in many parts of Canada, so a lot of people don't receive continuity of care. It is so valuable to have a doctor who knows your history. Family medicine takes into account the many factors that affect health, such as income, housing, and family relationships. Ali wanted to offer that kind of complete care.

Ali is one of the doctors on a family health team that also includes nurses, a nurse-practitioner, social worker, pharmacist, addiction counselor, and dietitian. She loves this model because the team members learn from one another. They share ideas and problem-solve together to give each patient what they need. It's good for patients and more fun for Ali than working alone, as some family doctors do.

Ali's team is able to help people with serious mental illnesses. This gives her the opportunity she originally wanted: to offer mental health care. Her other specialty is LGBTQ health. More than anything, she explains, this means being open-minded and not making assumptions. Things have improved a great deal in recent years, but queer and especially trans people can feel unsafe in health-care settings. Some doctors still misjudge who queer and trans people are and what they need.

In the field of medicine, it's important to think about and treat body parts regardless of who they belong to. This means understanding that a trans man might have a vagina, cervix, and uterus. A trans woman might have testicles.

They should receive the usual care for those body parts. Some trans men can get pregnant and may need contraception. It's not hard to understand once we adjust our thinking to separate sex from gender. And it shouldn't be hard to give the right care.

Still, some patients don't feel safe seeking treatment where they might be misunderstood or mistreated. Ali notes, "I still get a lot of reports of terrible experiences in emergency rooms or specialists' offices. When people are really in pain or in crisis, it makes them feel even worse. We still have a ways to go in making sure that all health-care providers have a basic level of respect and competency."

Ali CHARLEBOIS

- pronouns: **she/her**

- self-identification: **queer**

- **family doctor** who helps people with both physical and mental health

- passionate about **gender-affirming medical care**

One positive change is that family doctors can now care for patients who want to transition. The experience is very different from what Patricia Wilson went through nearly forty years ago. There is usually no reason to see a specialist, much less go through days of psychological testing. Family doctors can prescribe the hormones that help change their patients' bodies. They can also arrange for surgeries without having to send their patients for a special psychiatric assessment. The wait for these assessments used to cause long delays for treatment. If a medical practitioner feels they need more information to help a patient who is transitioning, they can get training through a program called Rainbow Health Ontario.

It's still true that many doctors don't really know much about trans health. What information they have may be outdated. Even when Ali was a student ten years ago, trans health was not covered in medical school. One of the other students had to organize extra training opportunities for those who were

GOOD MEDICINE: ALI CHARLEBOIS   **39**

interested. Health care has improved, thanks to efforts by trans people inside and outside the health-care system. Ali herself often trains medical students. Medical conferences are also giving more attention to trans health.

Activists are working to make sure trans people get what they need through their government or workplace health-care insurance without having to pay extra. Some procedures are considered elective and aren't covered, even though they feel very necessary to the people choosing them. For example, a woman who hasn't had much breast growth with hormones can't get free breast augmentation surgery but might really need it to feel comfortable. She might also want a procedure to reduce the size of her Adam's apple or to remove facial hair. These physical changes matter to many trans people. Without access to these procedures, they are more likely to be misgendered. Being misgendered hurts.

Ali is happy with her career choice. She says honestly, "Being a doctor is really hard. It can be grueling. But there's a lot of beauty to working in family medicine, being with people through their joys and challenges." She adds that, "Working with trans and nonbinary patients is some of the most meaningful work that I do. It's a privilege to play a role in helping people to feel comfortable in their own bodies and to be seen as who they are."

A LOT OF THINGS AT THE SAME TIME

SUZE MORRISON

Picket lines are great learning places for kids. My mom took me to picket lines during education strikes when I was a kid. Use it as a teaching moment. Talk about the history of the labor movement. Talk about the rights we have because of people that went on strikes before.

Suze Morrison was as surprised as anybody when she was elected to the Ontario Legislature in 2018. She was only thirty when she won the election and identifies as mixed Indigenous and settler and as bisexual. Everyone likes to talk about supporting and encouraging "diversity," but Suze didn't find many people like her in government. And being different from her colleagues, she discovered, would make her new job nearly impossible.

Suze grew up in what she calls an "activist-y" Toronto household, going to protests with her mom. But it was the activism of survival. Suze and her family had to fight for basic rights, like affordable housing, food security, and accessibility (her mom uses a wheelchair). Suze says that her family had to be activists just to get what they needed to live. She remembers going to the dentist for the first time in fifteen years after she got a job with health benefits. Before that, dentist appointments were a luxury Suze couldn't afford. She had seven cavities waiting to be filled. Many Canadians take these basic health-care necessities for granted.

After finishing university, Suze moved from Toronto to London, Ontario, a mid-sized city. Her activism grew to focus on her community rather than just her day-to-day needs. She got involved in efforts to stop police from "carding" people. All over North America, it is common for the police to stop people of color, especially young Black men, and ask them for identification. Often, the people are doing nothing wrong, minding their own business. This kind of harassment is so common that people say they were stopped for "driving while Black" or "walking while Black." It is totally unfair, and a clear example of racism.

Suze's next adventure was with a group in London working to get more women into politics. She began volunteering on election campaigns and learned about how government works at each level: municipal, provincial, and federal. In her twenties, she began to think that she might run for office down the road—maybe in ten or fifteen years when she had more experience. Meanwhile, she was working in the Friendship Centre movement, which offers culturally appropriate services and support to Indigenous people living in cities.

Suze returned to Toronto after her partner finished his studies. One night, they were coming home from a movie when they saw a young man lying on the sidewalk. Lemard Champagnie had been shot and left alone in the street, a victim of gang violence. They used their first aid knowledge to try to save him, but the young man died. It was a terrifying experience, and it shook her to her core. Suze was more determined than ever to help her community.

A few days later, the area's City Councilor, Pam McConnell, died. Suze had a lot of respect for Pam's work and was afraid that her replacement might not understand or particularly care about the needs of the community. In Suze's words, "We might get a dude bro in a suit who figures it's his time to shine."

Suze signed up for Campaign School, organized by Toronto City Councilor Kristyn Wong-Tam. She wanted to put her name forward to fill the opening left by Councilor McConnell. But before she could throw her hat in that ring, the New Democratic Party (NDP) asked her to run in the next provincial election. Suze thought going through the nomination process would be a learning experience and could help her better understand the political system. So, she ran to be chosen as the candidate in her downtown riding to represent the NDP in the next provincial election. She wanted to build relationships with more people in her community, but she didn't expect things to move so fast!

Suze MORRISON

- pronouns: **she/her**

- self-identification: **bisexual**

- elected to be a **Member of Provincial Parliament** at thirty

- works in the **Indigenous Friendship Centre** movement

She considered the whole thing a practice run. Before she knew it, she was walking into the Ontario Legislature as a Member of Provincial Parliament (MPP).

It was not a welcoming place. Not for a woman, not for a queer woman, not for a young woman, not for a part-Indigenous woman. Because Suze was not a member of the governing party, it was very difficult to make progress on the issues she cared about, particularly housing and youth services. This is true for any member of an opposition party. More than ever before, all over North America, conflict in politics is the norm. Politicians on opposing sides of an issue tend to dig in their heels. They could try to find common ground, but they don't want their opponents to succeed. There is little compromise or cooperation. It's not a useful way to govern because nothing gets done. It's not how any of us were taught to behave in day care and school. But what's different for a person like Suze is that few people even acknowledged that she belonged there. Time and time again, she was asked for identification while her older male colleagues waltzed through security. She was constantly asked, "Whose office are you from?" because people assumed she was an assistant to an MPP, not an MPP herself. After many months of this, she called the Sergeant at Arms, who is in charge of security. She asked that the security staff please learn to recognize her, so she could move through the government buildings with the same ease as her colleagues.

Despite the challenges, Suze persevered. She is proud to have saved a heritage building from illegal demolition. She went through all the formal channels in place to protect significant historic architecture. When that didn't work, she marched down to the site and stood in the way of the bulldozers. You would think an elected official with the political power and backing of her position wouldn't have to freeze her toes to fix a problem, but that's what she had to do. What Suze really wants to do is build affordable housing, protect tenants from rent increases and evictions, and invest in youth to prevent gun violence. These goals still require a big shift in priorities. Governments need to fund education and social services that give support and opportunities to low-income and racialized youth, not more policing to punish them after they've lost hope.

Suze is clear that the answer is not simply to bring more women or more people of different backgrounds into politics. She doesn't sugarcoat how hard the job is. The system is not designed with her in mind, because people like her weren't included in building it. The system needs to change. Otherwise, political newcomers will keep being pushed aside, questioned, and ignored. Would Suze tell her young self to get into politics? She's not sure. But she hopes things will change enough for today's girls to take their rightful place there. In a statement released in spring 2022, Suze announced:

> With the greatest mix of emotions, I want to share with you that I have made the difficult decision not to run in the June election. I need to step back for my health. I was diagnosed with endometriosis in 2019. My pain has worsened over the past two years. I'm doing well but being an MPP is a demanding role and I need to slow down for a while and get my pain under control.

Suze has returned to her previous work in a role with the Ontario Federation of Indigenous Friendship Centres. It's unfortunate to lose someone like Suze from a powerful political position. But health has to come first, and Suze is continuing to be a model to others by taking care of herself. To help with stress, Suze drives autocross, a timed competition where people maneuver cars solo around traffic cones on a specially designed course. It requires skill rather than speed or engine power, and Suze is a champion. She loves the feeling of control and excitement and feels very safe behind her own wheel.

In June 2021, Suze made the decision to come out as bisexual. She had been in government for three years by this time and married to a man for much longer than that. In an article for *NOW Magazine*, she explained:

I'm bi. While it's something I think I've always known, it took the space of endless lockdowns to come to terms with that label—and for me to figure out how to declare that identity while married. In the silence of my own apartment this past year, I realized I was finally ready to start using the right label for myself. I also realized that I have a responsibility to not only be honest with myself, but to the generation of queer and trans youth behind me—and to set an example for them that a 16-year-old version of myself could be proud of.

Sexual identity is more than who you love—it's who you are. Suze is able to say, "I'm a lot of different things at the same time, and that's good."

TALENT AND NERVE
DEBBIE SHEPPARD-CHESTER

My life has been kismet all the way through. I've been blessed.

From the time Debra (Debbie) Sheppard-Chester was little, she played with her brothers and the boys in her neighborhood. It never occurred to her that she couldn't do everything they could do. At Christmas, when she got a doll instead of the football she wanted, she was so disappointed. She thought it was unfair that Santa was punishing her when she'd been so good! Before she started junior high, her cousin Karen decided that Debbie needed a makeover. Until then, she'd been a happy tomboy, but Karen wanted Debbie to look and act like a girl, so she wouldn't embarrass her at their new school. Debbie went along with it. Because of the expectations put on women, the only future she could imagine for herself was as a wife and mother. She had only heard the word "queer" hurled as an insult. She didn't know any gay people, but she knew it was something to be ashamed of. Debbie had a high school sweetheart. Had he not broken up with her, she says, "I would have married him, had his babies, and been stuck in that town forever. That's how we were programmed."

When she finished high school, Debbie got the disappointing news that her parents couldn't afford to pay for her college. She had a bunch of siblings they needed to take care of. It was the early 1950s, and she lived in a small close-knit Cajun community in Texas. Walking in town with her friends one day, Debbie saw a sign at the US military recruiting office. It promised free tuition after a stint in the military. Debbie was smart and adventurous. She joined the navy on the spot.

At the time, gay, lesbian, bisexual, and trans people were not allowed to serve in the military. If they were discovered, they would receive a dishonorable discharge. Debbie remembers having to be so sneaky—the slightest hint that she was a lesbian would be enough to get her thrown out. A dishonorable discharge was considered a very shameful thing. And it would mean no tuition and no pension. It wasn't until 1993 that President Bill Clinton changed the policy to "Don't Ask, Don't Tell." This rule was confusing and cowardly. It basically said gay people were good enough to fight for their country but not good enough to deserve equal rights. Finally, in 2010, President Barack

Obama ended this discrimination. But the fight wasn't over. When President Donald Trump took office in 2017, he banned transgender people from the military. His completely made-up argument was, "They take massive amounts of drugs. They have to, and also, and you're not allowed to take drugs, you're in the military, you're not allowed to take any drugs." President Joe Biden overturned the ban in 2021. Queer rights in the military have changed under the last three presidents of the United States and remain uncertain.

When Debbie became a sailor with the US Navy in the late 1960s, she had little experience of the world beyond her hometown. She had never left Texas. She

Debbie SHEPPARD-CHESTER

- pronouns: **she/her**

- self-identification: **lesbian**

- was a member of the **US Navy** when queer people were not allowed to serve

- **worked in the trades** in all-male workplaces

did, however, know she was a lesbian. She had already had one girlfriend in secret. Not long after she left home, she came out to her group of six close friends—or, rather, they outed her. When visiting Debbie, they said, "Okay, enough of this. We know you're a lesbian and we love you." When she returned home after five years of military service, her childhood crew organized a camping trip and surprised Debbie by inviting her new gay friends. It's a memory Debbie cherishes to this day.

Debbie was entitled to her university tuition once she left the navy, but first she needed to make money. She was supporting herself and her family and had to delay her education. Her father had left her mother with kids still at home, and Debbie, the oldest, felt a duty to help her siblings.

Debbie moved around, always doing jobs that were considered nontraditional for a woman. One of her first civilian jobs was as a car "salesman." She

TALENT AND NERVE: DEBBIE SHEPPARD-CHESTER

saw an ad, needed a job, and went for it. She didn't think anything of it, but people were so surprised, they would visit the car dealership to see if it was true that a woman worked there. She was a local attraction!

For the most part, she worked in the trades—"on her tools," as she calls it. She was very talented with her hands and easily figured out how things worked. She apprenticed as a train engineer until she was laid off, then went to work as a mechanic. She got jobs in all-male workplaces because employers needed a token woman. The feminist movement was making it harder for companies to hire only men. A woman military veteran made them look even better. That didn't mean she was treated with any respect. She faced constant harassment. To cope, she thought of the guys who bothered her as just part of the furniture. Debbie made a point of being better at her job than they were.

Debbie had so much confidence, she once took a job as a boilermaker without having the faintest idea what a boilermaker did. She was in the employment office one day, looking for whatever general construction job she could get. Someone announced that they only needed boilermakers. Debbie changed her application form on the spot, claiming to have experience as a boilermaker (someone who installs and fixes boilers, which heat water). She was hired to start that very night. She quickly visited a friend who took her to buy the necessary tools and showed her how to use them. Now, that's nerve!

When Debbie finally had the chance to go to university, she was in her late thirties. She had taken care of her family and could pursue the dream she'd had since she was six years old: to be a pilot. She embarked on a seven-year journey sponsored by the Veterans Administration, earning a degree in aviation science and receiving her pilot's license. Maneuvering a plane through the sky was a thrill. She dipped and dove, "just like in the movies." She couldn't wait to spend the rest of her career as a pilot. Unfortunately, just after she qualified, a serious medical condition grounded her. She went to the doctor about her migraines and learned she had three large brain aneurysms. She was told not to bend over, much less perform loop-the-loops. Her flight career ended before it had even begun. Debbie was dismayed but her health had to take priority. Her situation was very serious, but she has defied the odds. Again!

Debbie has been happily married to her wife Glenda for twenty-seven years but has loved her for forty-three. They were the closest of friends for a long time before romance blossomed. Debbie came out to her mother while she was in the military. Her mother didn't want to talk about it, but at least the secret was out. The first time Debbie brought home a girlfriend, her mother was welcoming. Her father didn't accept Debbie for many years, and there was a lot of anger between them. He insisted that romance could only be between a man and a woman. He told Debbie, "Every woman I've ever been with has told me I was the best." Debbie said, "Well every woman I've been with has told me the same thing."

When Debbie's cousin Karen realized the truth, she was upset at first. Her mother said, "Karen, she's the same Debbie you've always known. What's different?" Karen had to agree. Debbie's aunt remembered that when she took them shopping as kids, Karen always turned toward the girls' section while Debbie headed over to the boys'. She had known the whole time. Now, Debbie is out to everyone and the beloved elder in her large extended family. She treats them to her amazing stories.

ACTING OUT
JO VANNICOLA

Even as a kid, I was always cast as a tomboy.

Jo Vannicola has been acting since they were a little kid in Montreal. They started dancing at the age of three, then moved into acting at just seven years old. They performed in local plays before they got a TV gig on *Sesame Street*. From there, their career took off—they got an agent and a manager and just kept going. The roles got bigger and better, and Jo earned their first (Canadian) Gemini Award nomination at the age of twenty-one. Jo won an (American) Emmy Award for a television film two years later.

Jo felt pushed into acting by their mother, but that's not to say they didn't enjoy it. Acting provided a creative outlet, a world of imagination, and a place to escape from a difficult home life. Jo experienced abuse and neglect from their parents. Jo would even say the arts saved them, filling their soul and opening up a powerful form of expression.

Jo moved to Toronto alone to attend a performing arts high school. They were all of fourteen years old and living independently. Their mother found them a room in an apartment and dropped them off there, only visiting occasionally. It was good for Jo to be out of their family home, but tough to grow up so fast and mostly alone.

When they came out as a teen in Toronto, there wasn't the same fear of family disapproval some people face, because they were already living on their own. Coming out was a significant decision in terms of their career, however. There were few representations of queer people on screen in the 1980s. The word "gay" was common, but Jo hadn't heard the word "lesbian" very often. There was barely language to describe nonbinary or trans people, or anyone who didn't fit a traditional male or female mold. Jo had not seen anyone they could identify with on TV or in movies. The few LGBTQ2 characters were often the butt of unkind jokes.

Shows like *Schitt's Creek* (which won nine Emmys!) have made LGBTQ2 characters more mainstream. But in the 1980s, Jo didn't know if they could ever be queer on camera. Jo was a young feminist and involved in social justice. They were vocal, rebellious, and carried a lot of anger about the trauma they had faced as a child. All of this fueled their commitment to making things better for queer actors and the queer community at large. Jo felt they had the fire—and stubbornness—to stick to their values. There were constant challenges. Jo was endlessly told to wear dresses to auditions, to put on makeup, and to grow their hair. In their twenties, Jo decided to stop agreeing to change their appearance. They also chose to be out. "It wasn't a horrible decision for me, but it did hurt my career. I had to deal with a lot of hostility. I'd say my appearance removes 80% of the acting work I might otherwise get."

Jo frankly states, "Someone could be lesbian but be very feminine and therefore play heterosexual roles and be fine with that. But I would not do that. That would be asking me to be a gender that I'm not." Instead, Jo found roles that did feel comfortable.

On *PSI Factor: Chronicles of the Paranormal*, Jo was one of the paranormal investigators—a bisexual character. This series, hosted by Dan Aykroyd, ran for four seasons in the late 1990s. On *Being Erica*, a television series that began in 2009, they played a lesbian character. "That was a role that I was requested to audition for."

More recently, Jo appeared in *The Expanse* on Amazon, a big budget, popular sci-fi drama. And in the fall 2022 pilot of the legal drama *Diggstown*, Jo played a trans character with a plotline involving the kind of negative treatment Ali Charlebois is fighting to change. Jo's character, a man named Morgan, is involved in a lawsuit against a doctor who sterilized him without his consent after performing a C-section. Morgan is a man who gave birth, but the judge in the show refuses to understand. She insists that Morgan is really a woman, because only women have babies. Unfortunately, the plot is very believable.

Jo VANNICOLA

- pronouns: **they/them**

- self-identification: **non-binary** and **queer**

- started **acting** at seven years old

- **writes** and **acts** to help tell LGBTQ2 stories

As a member of the Alliance of Canadian Cinema, Television and Radio Artists (ACTRA), Jo took the opportunity to push for change. They interviewed a number of other queer performers for an entertainment industry magazine. The article described the hurdles they have to clear to do the work they love. In 2018, Jo started outACTRAto, a committee within the union dedicated to knocking over these hurdles. The committee wrote a guide to working with queer actors to help educate producers, directors, and casting agents.

Very slowly, TV and movies have begun to better reflect the world. Jo is proud to have finally been able to play some queer characters, but they still represent a tiny fraction of the roles available to performing artists. There is a big difference between creating the occasional LGBTQ2 part for an actor and telling LGBTQ2 stories, which is why Jo writes plays and screenplays as well. "We're understanding that the door is shut. There is one tiny window open in the mainstream culture, and it's not big enough. So, we're creating our own content."

In 2021, Jo produced, wrote, and acted in a short film called *Trashed* that played the festival circuit. It's a labor of love, rather than a commercial project. "For me, it's about gaining experience and trying new things." Visibility is important. Young people need to see characters they can relate to—whether on screens or in books. More than that, they need to know the stories of past and present queer people from around the globe. Jo has received several awards for their advocacy work in this area. They have also written a memoir called *All We Knew but Couldn't Say*, which they hope to turn into a film or series.

For the next generation, Jo hopes there won't be any need for special committees to advocate for LGBTQ2 actors. Meanwhile, they would absolutely urge young people to dive into the arts, whether you want to act, write, or work behind the camera. If the entertainment industry and telling stories is where you decide to make your mark, there will be a place for you. And, unlike when Jo started out, the adults will have your back!

AN ALLY IN THE FIGHT AGAINST HIV/AIDS

DIDI CHARNEY

I signed up to volunteer at the AIDS hotline. I can see us in this room. There were maybe four of us. The referrals, if there were any, were written on pieces of paper. There was hardly anything.

Didi Charney was an actor in New York City when crisis struck the gay community. It was the mid-1980s, and nobody knew what was happening. Didi recalls, "I started hearing about people in my theater company getting sick. I started hearing stories that scared me. Pretty much everyone I knew who got HIV did die." Didi's instinct was not to run away, but to see what she could do. She had grown up in a family where it was expected that you support the people around you. There was a lot of social consciousness.

Didi volunteered for the very first AIDS Walk in 1986, which was all about awareness. There was so much misinformation and panic about the mysterious disease dubbed the "gay plague." Its original name was, in fact, Gay-Related Immune Deficiency (GRID). Once researchers learned that it was not gay-related, it was renamed AIDS. AIDS stands for Acquired Immunodeficiency Syndrome and is caused by the HIV virus. AIDS weakens the body's normal ability to fight illness. In the early days, people with AIDS were getting rare forms of cancer and other unlikely diseases. Some were dying of illnesses that are not usually serious among healthy young people, such as pneumonia. Today, there is still no cure but there are very effective medications. In countries where proper treatment is available, including Canada and the United States, patients can live long, healthy lives.

Back in the 1980s, governments were doing very little about the crisis. Because AIDS was affecting mostly gay men, a lot of people frankly didn't care. On top of that, gay men faced new levels of discrimination. Some were rejected by their parents, who only learned their sons were gay when they got sick. Many had to cope with the disease alone. People had not yet realized that AIDS could affect everyone; it just happened to be spreading in the North American gay community first. New York City was the worst hit. By the late 1980s, there were more than 10,000 new cases per year. At its peak in the mid-1990s, there were close to 10,000 deaths per year in the city alone.

Didi felt compelled to help. At the time, she was one of the very few straight women on the front lines of support efforts. She volunteered for the first AIDS hotline, educating herself as best she could to counsel people and make referrals to the services they needed. The first step was to explain how AIDS is transmitted. It is spread through body fluids: semen and blood. Education campaigns in the gay community focused on the importance of using condoms, which was not something gay men had usually done. Condoms are a crucial line of defense in keeping semen from entering another person's body.

Didi CHARNEY

- pronouns: **she/her**

- self-identification: **straight**

- **actor**

- was a dedicated **frontline volunteer** during the HIV/AIDS crisis

The hotline was operated by an organization called Gay Men's Health Crisis (GMHC). Didi spent many hours there in those early years and stayed for two decades. She was so committed that she would miss auditions to volunteer. Her dedication took a toll on her career, but she doesn't regret any of it. She found her work with GMHC very meaningful, even though it was emotionally difficult. Didi was there to offer comfort and support during the scariest, most uncertain moments of people's lives. Didi never took a paid job in the health field, but she maintains that being a volunteer gave her more than it took. Through this work, Didi made many close friendships; some were brief, as AIDS claimed more lives, but she cherished them.

In 1983, well-known playwright and activist Larry Kramer had left GMHC, angry that they weren't doing enough. He became one of the founders of Act Up in 1987, an organization focused on advocacy. Act Up was very political. Its purpose was to draw attention to "government negligence, social

AN ALLY AGAINST HIV/AIDS: DIDI CHARNEY **59**

neglect and the complacency of the medical establishment." GMHC was more involved in education and frontline support. Both were critically important. Kramer wrote *Normal Heart*, a play (now also a film) about those early days, when there was widespread panic about the issue.

Didi trained to become a peer group counselor and joined the speakers' bureau, traveling all over the city to educate people about HIV/AIDS. She visited corporate offices, informing people on how to protect themselves from getting sick and dispelling the myths about how the disease was spread. In the early days of HIV/AIDS, people were afraid to be anywhere near gay men. This fear continued long after it was understood that the disease could not be spread through the air or by touch.

Didi was a young straight woman. Her straight friends teased, "You're never going to meet somebody volunteering at an HIV/AIDS organization." But it so happened that she did meet the right guy while studying prison health at university. Her future husband came to her class as a guest lecturer. He was involved in an important lawsuit on behalf of inmates with HIV/AIDS. Wanting to learn as much as she could, Didi was taking master's level courses in public health. "You couldn't dabble when the problem was so critical," she explains.

Didi has attended every single AIDS Walk in New York City since 1986, walking 10 kilometers in and around Central Park. The early walks were small, but by the 1990s, they had grown to 50,000 people! Families took part, corporations got on board, and celebrities came to show their solidarity. More and more politicians appeared in public as attitudes changed. She says it was an extraordinary time that brought people together. "I can't say it was a party, because there was so much death, but there was such great solidarity and wonderful energy."

Didi remembers educating the police, while she was also busy stopping traffic as an event marshal. She never missed an opportunity to share facts with people who might have false information. Didi's son came along on the annual walk from the time he was in a stroller until he finished high school.

She continues to raise money for the AIDS Walk, which goes toward the care of people living with HIV and AIDS. Its focus has evolved; during the COVID-19 pandemic, support was directed toward the protection of HIV-positive people, who are much more vulnerable to illness, and helping them cope with isolation.

HIV/AIDS is now understood to be a disease that does not target any one group of people; that would make no scientific sense. It is spread mostly through sex. It can be transmitted to babies during pregnancy. It can also be spread via contaminated needles, harming drug users. Over the last forty years, AIDS has cost the lives of more than thirty-six million people worldwide. It is not under control in many countries. The hardest hit part of the world is sub-Saharan Africa.

In 2020, 680,000 people died of AIDS worldwide, and 1.5 million more people became infected with HIV. Where condom use is the norm, this number is lower. The widespread use of condoms is having added benefits, preventing other sexually transmitted diseases and unwanted pregnancies.

In recent years, Didi's acting career has taken an interesting turn. She often works in health-care settings, playing patients with different symptoms so that medical students can learn to diagnose illness and provide good "bedside manner." All her medical knowledge and volunteer experience are coming in handy.

DIGITAL DIVERSITY

RACHEL JEAN-PIERRE

It took time to feel ready to speak in public. I had to have a thick skin and be able to deal with ignorant questions.

Rachel Jean-Pierre pivoted from social work to tech, two seemingly unrelated fields that have one important thing in common: an understanding of human behavior. Rachel is a francophone Quebecer with Haitian roots. Living in Montreal, she works in digital marketing. She has always been involved in activism within the LBGTQ2+ community. After changing careers, she became a vocal advocate for women, queer people, and people of color in tech. In 2019, she was awarded a medal for her leadership by the National Assembly of Quebec.

But it took a lot for Rachel to accomplish what she has today. Back when Rachel finished school, she really wasn't sure what she wanted to do. She pursued fashion but soon learned how hard it is to make a living in that industry. She took women's studies, earning a bachelor's degree. An aptitude test pointed her toward law, so she took courses in criminology. Law school didn't pan out. Instead, she earned a master's degree in social work. Rachel had always been drawn to social justice and helping others and thought this would be a good fit.

Rachel became a social worker, first in Montreal, then she moved to a rural area in northern Quebec for a better job. In her new position, she worked in a health center that served all the needs of the community. This made her work interesting and more varied, but also exhausting. Social workers meet people when they are in crisis; they may be dealing with the death of a loved one, poverty, health problems, family breakdown, or abuse. Supporting people through these challenges is rewarding, but it's hard not to absorb some of their pain. Social workers are at very high risk for burnout.

Working such a stressful job in a place where she felt isolated, Rachel needed a change. She explains, "To move forward, my options were private practice or management, neither of which interested me." She had family and friends in tech industries, and Rachel had always done well in science, technology, engineering, and math (STEM). So, she returned to Montreal and started teaching herself the skills needed to break into digital marketing.

Have you noticed that after you "like" a post about something or search a topic in your browser, you start getting ads about it? For example, if you

64 PRIDE AND PERSISTENCE

look up dance classes in your area, you will start to see ads for dance camps, dance shoes, and all things dance-related wherever you go online. Digital marketers like Rachel figure out what you like and are looking for and send you related advertising. If you visit websites about New York, you might see ads for Broadway shows or the Guggenheim exhibits. This is where understanding human behavior comes in. The Internet allows advertisers to find the people who might want their product and target their ads to them. It's much better for business than paying for a billboard that will be seen by thousands of people who aren't the least bit interested.

Rachel JEAN-PIERRE

- pronouns: **she/her**

- self-identification: **queer/ lesbienne**

- **Fights for rights** of women, queer people, and people of color who work in technology

- started the Montreal chapter of **Lesbians Who Tech**

Rachel has a talent for this work and made a successful career switch. She started out in small companies, where her colleagues were often 95 per cent male and mostly white. It was the opposite of social work. She felt very alone as a queer Black woman. Rachel says, "In addition to paying the 'Black tax' (the cost to Black individuals of conscious and unconscious anti-Black discrimination), I couldn't bring my authentic self to work." Research shows that people who can't be themselves at work often feel anxious, stressed, and fatigued. Many workplaces now have Pride at Work or LGBT committees to help their employees feel safe and included.

When Rachel faced sexual harassment, she got no support. Her boss told her to avoid the guy who was harassing her. This was the absolute wrong response. It was also impossible to do with a staff of only fifteen people. She remembers, "For a year, I was being pinged by other companies, but I ignored the opportunities I was being offered elsewhere. And then the moment arrived." She quit.

In 2015, Rachel's sister told her about an international conference happening in San Francisco called Lesbians Who Tech. Rachel found her people there—thousands of queer women working in every imaginable job in technology! She was so inspired she started the Montreal chapter of Lesbians Who Tech. Rachel already had lots of experience as a volunteer activist. She had started a group for Black lesbians in Montreal and was involved in efforts to make the queer community more racially inclusive.

Lesbians Who Tech started meeting monthly, talking about their experiences, and inviting guest speakers on different themes. So many women wanted to connect, they would come from all over Quebec. Soon Rachel was invited to speak at conferences and events, promoting the benefits of a diverse tech workforce. She created a document called the "Women in Tech Manifesto" with a group of other women. It is full of tools, ideas, and speakers' lists that event organizers can use for their meetings and conferences. More than 500 people signed a pledge as part of this manifesto, promising to close the gender gap in ICT (information and communications technology). Among those who signed, one wrote,

> With an equal number of women on boards and in C-suites (executive positions), on stage and in the audience, it will change the ICT space much faster than anything else. I commit to act to aim for parity at technology events…and beyond.

Another noted, "More women in technology will make a difference in the value, growth, and success of companies. It makes sense and is the right thing to do."

Rachel has now moved to a huge international company in Montreal, with a staff that better reflects the real world. It also has clear policies about harassment and a proper process for reporting problems. If Rachel wants to keep challenging herself, this company has all kinds of different departments and clients with big budgets, so the sky's the limit. She is happy to report, "DEI (diversity, equity, and inclusion) is not a special project, it's in the DNA of the company. The work I used to do in the community, I can now do at the workplace."

The first time Rachel stood in front of an audience to talk about women in tech, her goal was simply to be visible. She was there to represent. "I wanted to give back what I didn't get." Rachel is a frequent guest speaker these days, and she always makes herself available to talk to the audience afterwards. She remembers when she felt too intimidated to reach out to prospective mentors. People approach her and tell her she's inspired them. "That's what keeps me going," she says. "It has purpose, and it brings value."

WE ALL NEED KINDNESS
FAITH NOLAN

I never thought of music as a career. I never imagined it was something I could do for a living. But, as a human being, I wanted to be heard and seen.

Faith Nolan calls themself an Afro-Scotian with Mi'kmaq and Irish ancestry. They were born in the late 1950s in Cape Breton, Nova Scotia, where their father worked in the coal mines. He played jazz guitar, and their mother played the drums. Music was part of their everyday lives. The mixed-race couple spent time in Africville on the outskirts of Halifax when they first got together. Interracial marriage was not illegal in Canada, but it was not accepted until several decades later.

Africville was a vibrant Black community with a history going back to the mid-eighteenth century. Faith compares it to Harlem in New York City; full of music and joy. It inspired their first album, *Africville*. The area thrived until the City of Halifax started expropriating its land for railway tracks, slaughterhouses, and garbage dumps that white people didn't want near their homes. Although the City collected taxes from Africville residents, it provided no municipal services. Halifax deliberately turned Africville into a slum, and then bulldozed it in the late 1960s. Residents were paid little or nothing for their homes and relocated against their will to terrible housing in Halifax. The racist destruction of this historic neighborhood has had a lasting impact on Black Nova Scotians. The city apologized for its actions in 2010.

The family moved to Toronto when Faith was a small child. Their dad had a job on TV, playing instrumental music on CBC—off-screen—when programming stopped at night. Imagine being able to tune in to live music if you couldn't sleep! Faith was always surrounded by music. Their mother rented out rooms in their house to help pay the bills. Musicians often stayed. One showed Faith how to pluck the strings of a guitar; another was short on rent, so he gave Faith's mother his guitar as payment. And Faith's career in music was born.

Folk songs were very popular when Faith was growing up and had a big influence on them. They realized music could tell all kinds of stories from the point of view of all kinds of people. They only remember seeing one Black woman who played guitar, Odetta, who was an American folk musician and

70 PRIDE AND PERSISTENCE

civil rights activist. Faith learned to play by ear, listening to their favorite records over and over again. They never imagined that music could be their job.

As a young teen, they started playing covers of folk songs during open mic nights at a nearby "hippie" café. Faith started to write music but wasn't ready to share it publicly yet. One day they played an original song for their mother. She became unusually quiet and still. Faith realized that music could get people to listen to you.

They began busking as a teenager. In only an hour one day, they earned fifty bucks, which seemed like a fortune. Playing was also soothing. "Music was a peaceful place to be," says Faith. It was a comfort during all the hours they spent alone, not part of the straight kids' social life. Twenty-one-year-old Faith was working at a factory when they discovered a bar with a big lesbian jam every Saturday. Faith was talented and charismatic—before long, they were invited to be its host. Then someone told them that the Holiday Inn hired musicians as "lounge lizards," playing in hotel bars.

Faith's first hotel gig was in Thunder Bay, Ontario. They traveled the province, playing six nights in one small town, then driving on Sunday to get to the next one. They had to learn every popular song of every genre to entertain the hotel patrons. After five years, Faith was tired of being on the road and performing other people's songs for drunken audiences who didn't really care who was playing. Sometimes men would shout over the music, "Hey, baby, take it off!"

Faith NOLAN

- pronouns: **they/them**

- self-identification: **queer** and **lesbian**

- wrote **Polaris Heritage Prize-winning album**, *Africville*

- **makes music** with teachers and union choirs

Faith got a job playing in Provincetown, a popular queer holiday destination in Massachusetts. It was liberating! For the first time ever, Faith felt they were part of the majority. They focused on writing music that meant something, starting with the songs recorded on *Africville*. Faith saw the opportunity to educate through music. In 2021, thirty-five years after its release, *Africville* was awarded the prestigious Polaris Heritage Prize for its contribution to Canadian music.

Faith approached schools to offer their services and was frequently given a small fee to give concerts and workshops that explored social issues through music. The Toronto District School Board even hired Faith to deliver more formal programming on race relations. It was meaningful work Faith was proud to do. On top of that, they continued to release albums and tour. Much to their surprise, they were making a living as a musician!

Faith sometimes played at Nolan's (no relation), a pub in Kingston, Ontario, where they met a guard from one of the women's prisons in the area. They received an invitation to play for the inmates. In the jail, Faith met Afro-Scotians who were all distant relatives of theirs, because the Cape Breton Black community is so insulated. Faith wanted to stay connected to these inmates and kept going back into the jail to play for them. They would sing with the women; sharing music and stories was an emotional experience for everyone. The women wrote the lyrics for an album Faith released called *Jailhouse Blues*.

At their home base in Toronto, Faith worked with a teachers' union to create a songbook in different languages, reflecting the music of many cultures. They led several union choirs. One highlight of this work was the creation of a ska album in collaboration with personal support workers. Called the CUPE (Canadian Union of Public Employees) Freedom Singers, this group played numerous festivals and even performed in Cuba. This kind of work brings a different set of rewards from performing as a solo artist; Faith finds it joyful and gratifying.

72   PRIDE AND PERSISTENCE

Now in their sixties, Faith is looking forward to some new post-pandemic inspiration. They've been jamming from time to time with people living on the street and are looking for a way to use music to support the efforts of housing advocates. Their whole body of work is about kindness and respect for everyone, no matter their circumstances.

We could all be weak, we could all be strong
We could all be right, we could all be wrong
We all need kindness, we all need love
Let's shine a light and be one love.

—Lyrics from "We're Different" by Faith Nolan

QUEER TANGO

ITZA GUTIÉRREZ ARILLO

In queer tango, you dance with people of different generations. It's about closeness, community, and making friends.

Itzayana (Itza) Gutiérrez Arillo grew up listening to tango music, but dancing was against the rules. It was considered sinful. They grew up in a very conservative Christian household in Mexico. Tango's melancholy lyrics matched their mood as a closeted queer teen. Itza found the music sad but soothing. They point out, "Most Latin American music features *penas alegres*—joyful sorrows." Tango was an outlet for their feelings. In English-speaking North America, we tend to think of tango as very romantic. It can be, but Itza explains that both the music and the dance are really about closeness and trust between any two people: friends, family members, or romantic partners.

After Itza moved to Montreal in their twenties for post-graduate studies, they discovered something called "queer tango." Itza could not have been more surprised to make this discovery *after* coming to Canada. By chance, at a birthday party, they met a couple of people involved in Queer Tango Montreal. They decided to try it out. "It was very scary, but it was a very healthy decision." They were thrilled to experience tango in a brand-new way.

In traditional tango, the man leads and is often presented as very dominant and confident. The woman follows and is seen as more decorative and passive, almost like his shadow. "It's what we call ESPN (or sports network) tango, very acrobatic with rigid gender roles."

When people start to learn queer tango, they learn the roles of both "leader" and "follower." Itza describes it as a conversation between two dancers— a conversation without words. The dancers are pressed up against each other, chest to chest and cheek to cheek. This closeness requires a great deal of trust. The two dancers move in unison and form an emotional connection. If one partner is feeling stressed or afraid, the other's energy and breath can help them relax. It's like dancing inside a big hug. Itza says, "I find it fascinating to carry on this silent negotiation with your partner."

People who take part in queer tango are a tight-knit community. They see one another at the same classes, dance parties, and festivals. Tango became popular in the 1930s and 1940s and traveled from Argentina and Uruguay to countries all over the world. Tango artists have always stayed in one another's homes when traveling or immigrating. This is also true for queer tango dancers, who often make close international friendships. This is one of the best parts, Itza notes. "You create a cosmopolitan network of friends—in Paris, Berlin, Buenos Aires, San Francisco—even if you only see them once a year."

As a child, Itza was taught that bodies are not for having fun. They had to relearn how to trust their body and relax. Itza slowly learned to let go, to move with someone else, and communicate without talking. Through queer tango, they also met other Spanish-speakers, which made them feel more at home. Now Itza sings and plays tango music on the guitar, dances tango, and teaches tango in their spare time. It fulfils their love of music, art, and performance.

Itza GUTIÉRREZ ARILLO

- pronouns: **they/them**
- self-identification: **queer**
- grew up in a conservative Christian home and **immigrated to Canada**
- dances **queer tango** in Montreal

They like to play old tango standards but add queer characters. The songs tell stories that combine joy and sorrow, comedy, and tragedy. Itza would say that tango has always been a little bit queer. By the time they embraced their own queerness, queer tango was becoming popular all around the globe. Some queer tango festivals last a weekend, others can go on for a whole week. They include instructors and dancers of all ages. One of the things Itza enjoys most about queer tango is the intergenerational participation. In South America, where tango comes from, it is usual for family members to dance together— little kids, adults, and elders alike. This is true for queer tango as well.

Tango parties are called *milongas*, a West African word that reflects the Black roots of tango. Queer tango milongas are organized by members of the queer community, but everyone is welcome to attend. Friends come to dance freely together. Queer people are also welcome at traditional milongas in Montreal and most cities of the world.

Itza feels that queer tango has really helped them overcome the trauma of their religious upbringing and their family's rejection. It has given their body a safe place, where touch can be good. Itza dances and sings tango with their queer friends of different ages, genders, and origins. Their strong and tender best friend has taught Itza that a hug can be calming. Their beautiful tango *maestro* has taught them the steps that allow them to dance without words. Their elegant elder *maestra* has taught Itza how to dance softly, like a happy starfish bobbing in the ocean. There is a word invented by their musical maestra to describe the joy of queer tango: "skinship." It expresses the feelings of comfort, closeness, and community this kind of dancing brings.

RUFFLING FEATHERS

TILLY KEEVEN-GLASCOCK

I wish this wasn't the thing that earned me my fifteen minutes of fame, but it hasn't soured me on activism.

Mathilda (Tilly) Keeven-Glascock is a student at Notre Dame, a private Catholic university founded in 1842 in the state of Indiana. Tilly is part of the LGBT student group on campus. You might have heard the expression, "Love the sinner, but not the sin." The Catholic church's view of homosexuality is this: Being homosexual is not a sin but acting on it is. LGBT people can belong to the Catholic church and even serve as clergy as long as they are celibate (straight clergy aren't allowed to have sexual relationships either). The group has only been allowed on campus since 2013, and it took a long, hard fight to get it approved. As Tilly says, "The campaign to get an LGBT group recognized on campus could be its own book."

Tilly enjoys her studies there and has made great friends. She does not, for the most part, feel excluded from campus life. She has rarely encountered any problems because of her sexuality. She changed direction once she got to Notre Dame. "I always wanted to be a teacher, but the summer before college, I thought I should do something more realistic and profitable, so I started out as a finance and economics major. I only lasted six weeks before switching to history and education."

Everything blew up in summer 2021. Tilly and two of her peers wrote an article for the student newspaper and started a petition opposing the opening of a Chick-fil-A restaurant on campus. Controversy follows Chick-fil-A wherever it goes. There are franchises all over the United States and a few in Canada. Chick-fil-A is known for its support of groups that oppose LGBT rights, particularly The Salvation Army and The Fellowship of Christian Athletes. CEO Dan Cathy has said that allowing same-sex marriage would "invite God's judgment" on the US. In response to protests and boycotts, the company has scaled back its support of these groups. But the company's owner and his family continue to privately fund anti-gay efforts. They are, of course, using money earned from selling chicken.

When Tilly and her friends decided to voice their arguments against the new Chick-fil-A, they did not for a moment believe they could stop it. "We just wanted to see if we could make some noise. At first, when the article appeared, nothing happened, which is what we expected. We got maybe two hundred signatures on our petition." They had hopes people would choose to eat elsewhere. Then things went berserk.

Tilly was writing an exam with her phone turned off on the day Fox News picked up the story about the students' opposition to Chick-fil-A. By the time Tilly turned her phone back on that evening, she had a ton of messages. The article in the little campus paper had gone viral. She remembers, "Late at night, I checked Twitter and immediately saw a weird message. It had an American flag in the profile picture and said, 'You stupid queers.' At first, I couldn't even think what it was about."

Fox News typically brings a very conservative bias to its reporting. It often takes an anti-gay position on stories. Tilly says, "When they can't find an actual news story, they scroll through the social media coming out of religious universities to see if they can find a controversy to write about. They've even reported on female students wearing leggings, which they feel are too provocative. They like to file almost any story under 'cancel culture.'"

Some of the messages were hateful. Tilly was living alone and was understandably scared. She was worried someone would find her address. She says, "You go off to college and feel like you're a grown-up, taking care of yourself. But I called my mom, and she came over. I was getting death threats. She brought a golf club."

> ## Tilly KEEVEN-GLASCOCK
>
> - pronouns: **she/her**
>
> - self-identification: **queer**
>
> - **university student** who plans on becoming a teacher
>
> - wrote **viral article** protesting Chick-fil-A coming to her campus

What really pushed things over the top was a Twitter thread the next day from Senator Lindsey Graham. Senator Graham announced that he would "go to war for the principles Chick-fil-A stands for." It generated hundreds of hateful comments directed at Tilly. She says, "Even though I had encountered homophobia in the past, there was something so targeted about this. They used my full name, and trolls said I was too stupid to go to Notre Dame, I must major in lesbian dance theory, I was a blue-haired liberal."

At the same time, though, social media users and media outlets had begun mocking Senator Graham. *The Washington Post* wrote:

> As a Senate member, Lindsey Graham has the ability to vote to send the United States to war. It's unlikely that a kerfuffle over a fast-food-chicken chain necessitating the deployment of troops would ever wind up before Congress, but on Thursday, the South Carolina Republican vowed that he would "go to war" to protect Chick-fil-A. Why might a purveyor of nuggets need such senatorial protection? A group of students at the University of Notre Dame had objected to the suggested opening of a location on its campus, citing the company's history of donating to anti-LBGTQ groups.

The story died down fairly quickly, but why did it even make the news? It wasn't as if there weren't other important things to report on. There was a pandemic going on. Incidents of racism were under scrutiny. Senator Graham didn't even represent Indiana. Tilly figures he wanted some attention that would rile up his supporters. He got what he wanted and made himself look like an idiot in the process.

Notre Dame did welcome Chick-fil-A, as expected. Nobody from the university ever responded to Tilly's reports about the death threats. Tilly questioned whether she would return to campus in fall 2021, but ultimately, she decided to continue her studies there. The negativity was from outside the campus and was outweighed by all the positive responses she received. She heard from former teachers, neighbors, and friends who all said, "If you've pissed off Lindsey Graham, you must be living your best life!"

Besides the huge amount of awareness this event caused, there was a concrete benefit. Tilly had the brilliant idea of asking supporters to donate $1 for every negative comment posted on social media. She opted to match hate with love. She raised $500 for The Trevor Project, a charity founded in 1998 to support suicide prevention efforts among lesbian, gay, bisexual, transgender, queer, and questioning youth.

Was it worth it? "Absolutely," says Tilly. "It taught me about activism and grassroots work. Every time I got a message to say 'I'm on your side,' it meant more to me than all those negative comments. Going forward, I think I'll treat myself with a little more care and gentleness. It's not going to stop me, it just might influence how I approach things in the future."

POST-PANDEMIC PRIDE

NATALIE MOORES

I always felt the guys at school acted silly and immature, and often I didn't share the same sense of humor. I would spend a lot of time thinking about things like a wedding, family...the whole "white picket fence" fantasy. I knew those things were pretty far from most guys' minds. I felt I needed to play with the other guys in the yard or on the court, but I just really wanted to be sitting in the grass with the girls talking about the topic du jour.

Before the pandemic, Natalie Moores had a pretty good life. She had a secure job, a solid marriage, a sweet baby son, and a nice house on a big lot in a small town west of Ottawa. Like all of us stuck at home during lockdowns, Natalie had a lot of time to reflect. She thought about how she'd spent the first four decades of her life and how she wanted to spend the next four.

Natalie was assigned male at birth. From an early age, she knew she wasn't quite like the other boys. She felt more at ease with girls. As a teen, she made an effort to hang out with boys, as was expected. She knew she wasn't gay—she was definitely attracted to girls. But she lived with depression and had the sense something wasn't right. Then, one night in spring 2021, she suddenly figured out what it was.

Natalie had never felt a need to express her femininity before, but during the pandemic, she felt free from the usual rules. She worked at home, and with salons closed, she let her hair grow long. One night, catching her reflection in the bathroom mirror, she saw Natalie looking back at her. Thinking back on that life-changing moment, she says:

> Seeing Natalie was definitely unexpected, but I must have been prepared to allow my reflection to finally register in that way. In a matter of seconds, I was flooded with memories of all the times I had questioned my true nature. Suddenly I had answers and a valid explanation of what I was actually feeling during each of those times. I felt a huge sense of relief and excitement.

The next morning, Natalie told her wife what had suddenly become crystal clear to her: She is a woman, and she is a lesbian.

Natalie felt a powerful urge to start her journey to learn about herself. She was also afraid she might lose everything, but her wife was very supportive. She even bought her a cake with the trans flag on it to mark her "rebirthday." Yet, despite their love and commitment for each other, their romantic relationship ended. Now, their family is figuring out their new structure, still cohabiting and co-parenting. They are giving it time, waiting with open hearts to see what comes next.

For Natalie, being her true self means there are new sources of joy every day. Some are small—she's glad not to have to pretend to enjoy sports anymore! Some are huge— her son's day-care staff call her "Maja" (a nickname she made up) instead of "Dad." Each step that moves her forward in her journey is a thrill, even shaving her legs for the first time.

In the easygoing way of young children, her son has taken this change in stride and has no trouble with her pronouns. The reaction of her family has been much better than she imagined. Natalie's mother enjoys fashion and goes shopping for clothes and makeup with her.

Natalie MOORES

- pronouns: **she/her**

- self-identification: **trans woman** and **lesbian**

- advocates for **trans health-care access** and coverage for transition-related care

- attended her first pride events and joined her local pride society after **coming out during the COVID-19 pandemic**

In the small town where she lives, Natalie has felt more nervous. It's not easy to go into the local hardware store as her new self, though she says the long pause of in-person activities caused by COVID-19 actually helped. She was able to tell friends and colleagues about her transition before seeing them in person. Natalie has ventured out slowly and found safe spaces to get coffee, shop, and enjoy a night out. She has wasted no time finding other trans people in her local area and in nearby Ottawa.

Natalie has jumped in with both feet, now that in-person events are back, and people are gathering again. She accepted an invitation to join Arnprior

Pride's planning committee, which organized its very first events to run throughout summer 2022. They held a scavenger hunt, bingo game, bowling night, and a couple of drag shows, which drew good crowds. Drag shows are fun, and Natalie feels they gently nudge people toward acceptance of gender nonconformity and create a safer space for her.

Natalie took the week off work to attend Capital Pride in Ottawa at the end of August 2022. It was her first big Pride event, and she was looking forward to taking it all in. "It took me decades to find a sense of pride in myself, so I'm excited to show my true colors with the world around me."

Natalie has joined several groups to find support and community, including her local PFLAG chapter (originally called Parents, Families, and Friends of Lesbians and Gays, but now just PFLAG) and a trans group that meets through Kind Space, an Ottawa community organization.

Natalie has already found the courage to advocate for better trans health coverage at her workplace. She is a computer network administrator in the federal civil service. Because only "top" and "bottom" surgeries (to reshape the chest and genitals) are covered by most provincial government health plans, trans people have to pay for everything else. As Ali Charlebois explains in her story, many trans people need other procedures to look and feel good. Natalie could not agree more that gender dysphoria (unease caused by a mismatch between biological sex and gender identity) is a serious health issue. Some trans people go to great lengths to find the money for treatments, such as voice modification therapy or facial feminization.

As of 2022, only the Yukon Territory covers a full range of gender-affirming treatments through its government health plan in Canada. Yukon's policy explains, "Delaying or denying access to transition-related health care can cause significant harm, and research has demonstrated that completing a transition for those who need it can considerably increase a person's well-being." While other governments catch up (we hope), some private health insurance plans do cover more gender-affirming treatments. Most big workplaces

88   PRIDE AND PERSISTENCE

offer their permanent staff extra health benefits on top of their wages. Natalie learned that her insurance company does, in fact, offer full coverage, but the Government of Canada does not provide this package to its employees. Natalie has joined the Gender Identity and Expression Action Committee at work, which is lobbying to get these benefits for all federal employees. Being part of this committee is teaching Natalie a lot about how to work the system. She's fighting for what's right, while gaining mentors and friends at work.

She has felt compelled to get involved because she feels the trans community has to defend their right simply "to exist the way we were born." The first step is to correct the misinformation that fuels discrimination. Natalie notes,

> Finding that strength isn't easy, particularly during times where I need to focus most of my energy on the needs of my evolving family and my transition. But at the end of the day, not only do I want to work to contribute to positive progressive change for my community, but I also want to grow stronger by learning from role models that are already accomplishing amazing things.

Now in her early forties, Natalie says the best time to transition would have been twenty years ago, "but the second-best time is now."

CONCLUSION

When we speak, we are afraid our words will not be heard or welcomed. But when we are silent, we are still afraid. So it is better to speak.

—Audre Lorde

As the stories in this book have shown, speaking up can be hard but very much worth the risk.

If Tilly hadn't spoken out against Chick-fil-A, she never would have raised $500 for The Trevor Project (and made Senator Lindsey Graham a laughing-stock as an added bonus). If Ali hadn't thought to herself, "I don't want to provide health care that only the rich can afford," she wouldn't be doing the important work she does as a family doctor. If Susan hadn't said to the judges of the Supreme Court, "Think of the children," the banning of books with queer characters might have gone on much longer, leaving lots of kids feeling left out and perhaps even alone in their classroom.

It can sometimes feel as if any movement for change involves two steps forward and one step back. Or even one step forward and two steps back, as battles that were already won have to be fought all over again. In North America right now, we're seeing a backlash against women's rights and queer rights, and it's frustrating. I have a placard in my front hall closet that I pull out regularly to go to one rally or another. It says, "I can't believe I still have to protest this shit!"

At the same time, I think about the massive changes that have happened just in my lifetime. Being queer in Canada has gone from illegal to accepted to celebrated. Even five years ago, if someone had told me nonbinary characters would be on prime-time TV, I'd have dismissed it as wishful thinking.

Each small nudge toward fairness for all really does lead to more small nudges, one after another, that move change along. What's especially exciting for me, as a lesbian feminist of sixty, is that young people have taken the baton passed to you from my generation, and you are running with it at speeds that blow my mind. You are so open-minded, thoughtful, and accepting of difference. I know you are also hopping mad about a lot of things, as you should be. There is much still to do. And you will be the ones to do it.

Never doubt that a small group of thoughtful, committed citizens can change the world; indeed, it's the only thing that ever has.

—Margaret Mead

GLOSSARY

This is not meant to be a complete queer glossary; there are other words that have to do with queerness and these definitions are not a final understanding of them. Many of these terms have changing definitions and are used differently by different people in the queer community. This glossary is meant to help readers understand the concepts and identities talked about in this book and to provide a jumping-off point for people wanting to learn more.

2SLGBTQIA+/LGBT/LGBTQ+: Two-Spirit, Lesbian, Gay, Bisexual, Transgender, Queer or Questioning, Intersex, Asexual, and more. This book uses many different acronyms to reflect the different language used by each person interviewed.

Activist: Someone who fights for social or political change and makes the world a better place. The people in this book are queer activists, each in their own way.

AFAB/AMAB: Assigned Female At Birth/Assigned Male At Birth. These terms separate the sex someone is assigned at birth based on their body parts from their gender identity. Sex and gender do not always line up. For example, someone might be assigned male and assumed to be a boy, but they may realize they are actually a girl.

Ally: Someone who supports, celebrates, cares for, and stands up for members of the queer community.

Aromantic: People who do not usually experience romantic attraction to others. However, sexuality is a spectrum, so aromantic people can still have romantic feelings. This term is often shortened to "aro."

Asexual: People who do not usually experience sexual attraction to others. However, sexuality is a spectrum, so asexual people can still experience sexual feelings. This term is often shortened to "ace."

Bisexual: Someone who is attracted to girls and boys or women and men.

Butch: Someone who presents their gender in ways that society sees as masculine. This term is especially important in lesbian culture and history.

Cisgender: Someone whose sex identification when they were born continues to feel right as they grow up.

Coming Out: Coming out, or coming out of the closet, means telling someone what your sexual or gender identity is. Coming out does not just happen once; queer people have to grapple with how to come out on an ongoing basis. Some choose to be out to some people in their lives but not to others, and some choose never to come out.

94 PRIDE AND PERSISTENCE

Dead Name: The name that a transgender person had before transitioning to their correct gender. It is offensive to call a transgender person by their dead name.

Discrimination: To discriminate against someone is to treat them differently and unfairly because of a part of their identity, which could include race, gender, sexuality, age, disability, religion, etc. 2SLGBTQIA+ people still face discrimination all over the world.

Dykon: A slang term for a lesbian icon. Many of the people in this book are dykons.

Femme: Someone who presents their gender in a way that society sees as feminine. This term is especially important in lesbian culture and history.

Gay: Usually used to describe men who are attracted to other men, the word gay has also become an umbrella term for people of any gender who are attracted to people of the same gender as them.

Gender Dysphoria: A feeling of pain and stress that people have when their gender identity is different from the gender and sex that they were assigned when they were born.

Gender Euphoria: A feeling of happiness and comfort when someone's gender identity is validated by other people and when they can express their gender in a way that feels right to them.

Gender Expression: The ways that someone expresses their gender outwardly. This could be through clothing, voice, behavior, pronouns, names, etc. Sometimes, the way that people express their gender to other people is different from how they feel inside.

GLOSSARY   95

Gender Identity: Gender is about how you feel and identify, while sex is about what body parts you have. A person's gender identity is their understanding of themself as a boy, girl, nonbinary person, Two-Spirit person, genderqueer person, or any other identity on the gender spectrum.

Genderqueer/Gender Fluid/Gender Nonconforming/Agender: Someone who does not conform to the expectations that come with being a boy or girl and who does not feel exactly like a boy or a girl.

Heteronormativity: The ideas and attitudes in society that hold up the idea that being straight and cisgender is the more "normal" way to be, and it is better than being queer. Heteronormativity contributes to the oppression of queer people.

Heterosexual/Heteroromantic: Someone who is only attracted to people of a different gender from them. For example, a girl who is only attracted to boys is heterosexual.

Homophobia: Hatred of and discrimination against homosexual people.

Homosexual/Homoromantic: Someone who is only attracted to people of the same gender as them. For example, a boy who is only attracted to boys is homosexual.

Lesbian: A girl who is attracted to other girls.

Nonbinary: Someone whose gender identity is outside of the categories of male and female or boy and girl. Nonbinary gender exists on a spectrum, which means nonbinary people may feel partly like a boy and partly like a girl, or they may feel like both, or neither, or somewhere in between.

Oppression: When a group of people who hold power in society use it to control and discriminate against a group of people who have less power. 2SLGBTQIA+ people have experienced and still do experience oppression all over the world.

Outing Someone: To tell others about someone's sexuality or gender identity. Outing someone can be harmful and dangerous. People should always be allowed to choose for themselves if, when, or how to come out to others.

Pansexual: Someone who is attracted to people regardless of their gender. Pansexuality is different from bisexuality because gender does not factor into their attraction.

Passing/To Pass: When a queer person can go unnoticed and not be visibly part of the queer community. People who pass as straight or cisgender often experience less discrimination.

Pronouns: The words we use to refer to someone based on their gender. Some examples of pronouns are he/him, she/her, they/them, ze/zir.

Queer: Often used as an umbrella term for all members of the 2SLGBTQIA+ community.

Questioning: Someone who is not sure of or is still in the process of discovering their gender or sexuality.

Sexuality/Sexual Orientation: People's experience of romantic and sexual attraction to others. There are many different sexual orientations, including gay, straight, lesbian, bisexual, pansexual, asexual, and others.

Spectrum Model: Many people believe that both sexuality and gender exist on a spectrum. The word spectrum comes from light, where the colors of the rainbow blend into one another. A spectrum of sexuality and gender helps to explain that many people do not feel they neatly fit into one specific category: Some people are not straight or gay, boy or girl, but somewhere in the infinite variety of shades in the middle. It is okay not to fit exactly into a category, and it is okay not to know. Some people feel that categories and labels help them understand their identity and experience. The important thing is to be inclusive of however a person understands themself.

Trans Man: A man who identifies as transgender.

Trans Woman: A woman who identifies as transgender.

Transgender: Someone whose gender identity does not match the sex they were assigned when they were born. This term is often shortened to "trans."

Transitioning: The process of going from the gender you were assigned when you were born to the gender that you truly are. It often involves changes in the way you express your gender to other people, like choosing a different name and pronouns, or making changes to the way you speak or dress. It can also involve gender-affirming procedures like hormone therapy or surgery, but not always. There is no right way to transition, and some transgender people are unable to or choose not to transition.

Transphobia: Hatred of and discrimination against transgender people.

Two-Spirit (2S): Used by Indigenous Peoples in North America to describe queer identities that are not part of the way Western and colonial societies usually understand sexuality or gender. Two-Spirit can refer to different things by different Indigenous communities.

ACKNOWLEDGMENTS

I'd like to thank Gillian Rodgerson for first suggesting I try writing for a younger audience, and Jordan Ryder for seeing this project through with me, as well as the many skilled readers who provided editorial suggestions. Thanks also to Lydia Derry for putting together a young test audience and to the following for their enthusiasm and feedback: Elsie Alfred, Roxie Chai, and Amalia Costa.

I am especially grateful to all the people who shared their stories so openly with me and allowed me to include them in this book.

I appreciate the work of all the activists before me who made it possible for me to come out in my late thirties without causing any kind of stir whatsoever.

Funding support for this project was provided by the Canada Council for the Arts and the Toronto Arts Council.

ABOUT THE AUTHOR

Mary Fairhurst Breen is the author of the memoir *Any Kind of Luck at All*, the picture book *Awesome Andie's Best of the Block*, and numerous magazine and newspaper articles and nonfiction stories. As a queer feminist author, writing is Mary's current form of activism, after decades spent working for social change and protesting for equal rights. She lives in Toronto.